AR PTS: 1.0

20TH CENTURY DESIGN

40s & 50s

WAR AND POSTWAR YEARS

For a free color catalog describing Gareth Stevens Publishing's list of high-quality books and multimedia programs, call 1-800-542-2595 (USA) or 1-800-461-9120 (Canada). Gareth Stevens Publishing's Fax: (414) 332-3567.

Library of Congress Cataloging-in-Publication Data available upon request from publisher. Fax: (414) 332-3567 for the attention of the Publishing Records Department.

ISBN 0-8368-2707-4

This North American edition first published in 2000 by
Gareth Stevens Publishing
A World Almanac Education Group Company
330 West Olive Street, Suite 100
Milwaukee, Wisconsin 53212 USA

Original edition © 1999 by David West Children's Books. First published in Great Britain in 1999 by Heinemann Library, Halley Court, Jordan Hill, Oxford OX2 8EJ, a division of Reed Educational and Professional Publishing Limited. This U.S. edition © 2000 by Gareth Stevens, Inc. Additional end matter © 2000 by Gareth Stevens, Inc.

Picture Research: Brooks Krikler Research
Editor: Clare Oliver
Additional Research: Nesta Fitzgerald

Gareth Stevens Senior Editor: Dorothy L. Gibbs
Gareth Stevens Series Editor: Christy Steele

Photo Credits:
Abbreviations: (t) top, (m) middle, (b) bottom, (l) left, (r) right

Braun (courtesy): page 25(tr).
Corbis: Cover (tl, bl, r), pages 3, 4-5, 5(t), 6-7, 8(b), 9(all), 10(t), 11(tl, tr), 12(both), 12-13, 13(t, m), 15, 16(t), 16-17, 17(both), 18(both), 18-19, 19(all), 20(t), 20-21, 21(all), 24(b), 25(l, br), 26(both), 27(r), 28(br), 29(l).
Mary Evans Picture Library: page 4.
Hulton Getty Collection: Cover (lm, rm), pages 6(l), 11(b), 14(tl, tr), 16(m, b), 20(b), 22-23, 28(tr), 29(tr, b).
Philip Jarrett: pages 14-15.
Kobal Collection: pages 5(m, b), 23(tl), 28(mr).
Pictorial Press: pages 26-27.
Science & Society Picture Library: pages 24(l), 27(l).
Frank Spooner Pictures: pages 6(b), 7(t, b), 8(t, m), 10(b), 10-11.
Vitra Design Museum: Cover (ml), pages 22(both), 23(tr, br).
© Vogue/Condé Nast Publications / Carl Erickson: page 28(bl).

Printed in Mexico

1 2 3 4 5 6 7 8 9 04 03 02 01 00

20TH CENTURY DESIGN

40s & 50s

WAR AND POSTWAR YEARS

Helen Jones

Gareth Stevens Publishing
A WORLD ALMANAC EDUCATION GROUP COMPANY

CONTENTS

During the war, people had to "make do and mend" to conserve scarce resources.

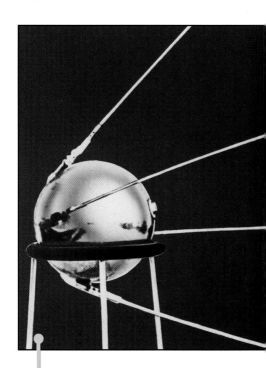

The USSR's launch of the first satellite, Sputnik 1, in 1959, marked the beginning of the space age. It was one of the greatest technological milestones of the century.

WAR AND PEACE

The 1940s began with a terrible war in Europe that called for every available resource and prompted the development of many new technologies.

Desperate shortages created by the war continued into peacetime, and, until more resources were available, austere designs continued, too. As economies gradually recovered, large quantities of goods were mass-produced at low prices, sparking a consumer revolution.

The 1950s brought a general feeling of optimism. New buildings were constructed. Teenagers wore the latest fashions and bopped to the newest sounds. Families bought cars and television sets. Car ownership grew so dramatically that planners had to redesign roads and cities. With the development of jet airliners, foreign travel also increased.

Throughout the 1950s, pioneer designers, such as Raymond Loewy and Le Corbusier, promoted the principles of good design until manufacturers and governments understood its importance. As the decade ended, designs had grown from functional to futuristic.

Wartime bombing reduced many European homes and architectural landmarks to rubble. Postwar rebuilding was a major project.

Pop stars, such as Elvis Presley, influenced teenage tastes, especially in music and fashion.

American cars of the 1950s featured exaggerated "fins." (1959 Chevrolet Impala)

INFORMATION GRAPHICS

During the war, artists, illustrators, and graphic designers used their skills to design propaganda materials. Later, they used the same techniques to promote products and companies.

The Utility logo, designed in 1942, used simple shapes to visually present the functional range of goods.

POSTER POWER

Wartime posters urged people to join the army or gave them instructions, such as how to wear a gas mask. Other posters were propaganda, intended to inspire patriotism. Britain's official poster artist, Abram Games (1914–1996), liked to use memorable sayings, such as "Careless Talk Costs Lives."

POSTWAR SYMBOLS

After the war, designers continued to use symbols to represent ideas in a catchy way. For example, the logo for the 1951 Festival of Britain was carefully designed with Union Jack colors and the head of Britannia to inspire pride in the nation.

Abram Games's logo for the 1951 Festival of Britain featured a stylized Britannia over a semicircle of blue, white, and red flags.

FATHER OF DESIGN

French-born designer Raymond Loewy (1893–1986) was a pioneer of good design. Working in the United States, he recognized the growing sophistication of consumers and advised manufacturers to entice their customers with elegant, streamlined designs. To the delight of the manufacturers, Loewy's strategy worked.

In 1949, Loewy became the first designer to be pictured on the cover of Time *magazine. The caption read, "He streamlines the sales curve."*

TWENTY CENTS OCTOBER 31, 1949

TIME

THE WEEKLY NEWSMAGAZINE

DESIGNER RAYMOND LOEWY
He streamlines the sales curve.

Swiss-born typographer Adrian Frutiger designed the Univers typeface in 1954. Univers was an instant success. Its simple lines gave it an ultramodern look. Univers was one of the first sans-serif typefaces.

ABCDEFGHIJKL   UVWXYZ a

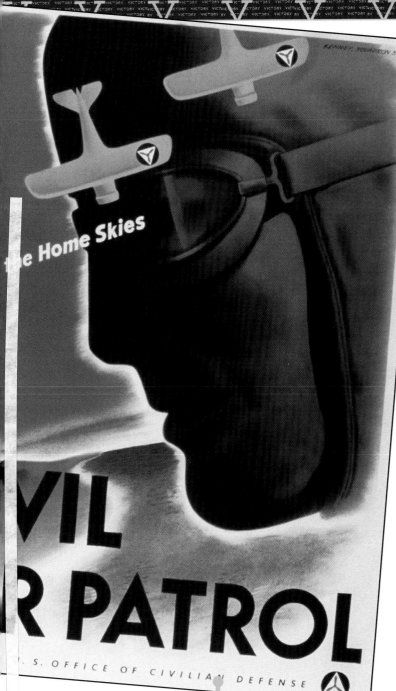

the Home Skies

VIL
R PATROL

U. S. OFFICE OF CIVILIAN DEFENSE

This poster was used by the U.S. government in 1943 to reassure people of their safety. It features easy-to-read, sans-serif type and cheery, patriotic colors.

LUCKIES
AMERICAN BLEND

LUCKY STRIKE
IT'S TOASTED

FILTERS

Loewy used bold, sans-serif type and an eye-catching bull's-eye to redesign Lucky Strike packages in 1940–1942. This package design has remained the same for the past sixty years.

LONG-TERM LOGOS

As companies began to realize the power of brand names, they commissioned designers to create unique logos for their products. They hoped the logos would make products easy to recognize and attract loyal customers. Paul Rand's logo for IBM, designed in 1956, was one of the longest lasting symbols of corporate identity. Its clear design showed Rand's ability to break a logo down into simple, timeless shapes.

Loewy's logos used basic shapes. His timeless designs are still recognizable today.

SIMPLE TEXT

The text of this book is printed in a serif typeface with decorative strokes on the letters. In the 1940s and 1950s, typographers felt that the clean lines of sans-serif typefaces, such as Univers, without decorative strokes on the letters, were more modern.

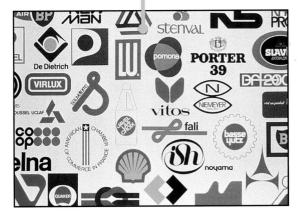

cdefghijklmnopqrstuvwxyz 1234567890

WARTIME TECHNOLOGY

Faced with the urgent demands of war, scientists and engineers developed technologies such as nuclear power and computers. Some of the greatest technological advances, however, were in aviation.

Curtiss planes were some of the first to be built entirely of stressed metal. The symbolic artistry of ancient warriors inspired this paint job.

HIGH FLYERS

As nations battled for air supremacy, military planes developed rapidly. Engineers produced faster fighters, bombers, and spy planes, but their progress was hindered by limited resources. The 1942 American fighter plane *Kittyhawk*, for example, did not fly as fast as it could have because the turbo-superchargers it needed to boost its engine were scarce and were allocated to bombers, instead. Even so, *Kittyhawk*'s engine was twenty times more powerful than the engine of a modern family car!

From 25,000 feet (7,600 meters), flying at a speed of about 186 miles (300 km) per hour, Boeing's B-17 Fortress could drop 4,000 pounds (1,800 kilograms) of bombs.

ROCKET SCIENTISTS

On October 3, 1942, the Germans successfully launched an A-4 long-range missile known as the V2, or Vengeance Weapon 2. The V2 was the first space rocket ever launched, and it successfully hit its target 119 miles (192 kilometers) away.

COMPUTER AGE

Colossus, a British-built computer completed in 1943, was as long as four buses. It was used to decipher codes created by the German machine, Enigma. After the war, when scientist John von Neumann suggested using binary codes to store information, computers got smaller!

A U.S. computer for building missiles (1950)

After the war, German engineers went to the United States with enough material to make one hundred V2s. A V2 rocket was launched in New Mexico in October 1946.

8

Fueled with alcohol and liquid oxygen, the V2 reached its target speed of 3,418 miles (5,500 km) per hour in about one minute. Then, the motor stopped, and the rocket continued toward its target in a free fall. Germany built more than 6,000 V2s. This amazing missile was the forerunner of modern guided missiles and of all rockets used in space launches.

DAWN OF THE NUCLEAR AGE

Splitting the nucleus, or center, of an atom of a heavy element, such as plutonium or uranium, is called nuclear fission. Nuclear fission releases a huge burst of energy, or nuclear power. The United States dropped the first nuclear bombs on the Japanese cities of Hiroshima and Nagasaki in 1945. The uranium bomb dropped on Hiroshima flattened 3.9 square miles (10 sq km).

Models of Little Boy *and* Fat Man, *the bombs dropped on Hiroshima and Nagasaki in 1945*

After the war, the United States completed more nuclear testing, which included dropping an atomic bomb near Bikini Atoll in the Pacific in 1954.

Nuclear power is also used to fuel submarines and to provide a renewable source of energy for homes. The first commercial nuclear power plant opened in 1956 at Britain's Calder Hall.

Atomic test at Bikini Atoll in 1954

ON THE ROAD

During the war, gasoline was in short supply and had to be rationed to consumers. In fact, in Britain, gasoline remained rationed until 1954. So, for most people in the 1940s, owning a car was an unaffordable luxury.

INDIVIDUAL FREEDOM

During the 1950s, as average incomes rose and fuel supplies became more available, more people both in Europe and the United States bought cars. For Americans, especially, having the freedom of the open road came to symbolize all kinds of hopes and dreams. To reflect this excitement and optimism, car manufacturers produced futuristic designs.

10

Pointed metal tail fins typified the showy styling of the big American sedans. (1957 Chevrolet Bel Air)

Convertibles, such as this 1950 Studebaker designed by Raymond Loewy, became a symbol of youth and glamour.

SHOWING OFF

Exaggerated styling became the new look, and cars were designed with shiny chrome fins and high front ends to suggest speed. With two headlights for eyes, a grille for a nose, and a fender for a mouth, a car's facelike quality made it seem like a loyal friend — with its own personality!

The 1956 Messerschmitt Cabin Scooter was one of many European attempts to design a miniature town car. It was inexpensive, but not versatile.

SMALL IS BEAUTIFUL

While American cars grew bigger, Europeans designed more economical forms of private transportation. In Britain, France, and Germany, fuel-efficient vehicles such as bubble cars, tricycles, and motorcycles were perfect for city driving.

SCOOTING AROUND

Motor scooters were particularly economical because they used very little gasoline. The Italian firm Piaggio began selling the Vespa in 1946 and kept it in production for more than forty years. The elegant little Vespa was inexpensive to run and easy for both men and women to drive. Its greatest competitor was the Lambretta, which came out in 1947.

PUBLIC TRANSPORTATION

Of course, not everyone had private transportation, so buses and streetcars were still popular. America's famous Greyhound buses traveled coast to coast. Redesigned by Raymond Loewy in the 1940s, the Greyhound bus became a postwar design icon.

Although its top speed was only about 30 miles (50 km) per hour, the Vespa was ideal for traveling on 1950s city streets.

THE GODDESS

The Citroën DS (short for *déesse*, or "goddess") stunned the automotive world with its many futuristic features. While earlier cars relied on springs to cushion a bumpy ride, the DS used a new system of water pressure, called hydropneumatic suspension. Its aerodynamic body allowed the DS to turn corners at high speed without tipping. Even the rear window was specially styled — angled so it would not need a windshield wiper!

The Citroën DS was unveiled at the 1955 Paris Motor Show.

Loewy's streamlined, curvy redesigns for the Greyhound Bus Company gave its coaches a recognizable identity.

TRANSPORTATION OF THE FUTURE

With the war behind them, designers were optimistic about the future. Anticipating the space age, they designed prototypes for the transportation of the future. Few of these prototypes were actually produced, yet they had an influence on later designs.

In 1954, Ford built this futuristic prototype out of blue and red pearlized plastic.

SELF-DRIVING CARS

With private cars becoming an increasingly important form of travel, American industrial designer Norman Bel Geddes (1893–1958) suggested that cars of the future would drive themselves along color-coded roads! By the end of the century, this prediction would come true, but with satellites, rather than colored roads, controlling the cars.

TUCKER'S LUCK

In 1948, American Preston Tucker started a company to sell his revolutionary car, the "Tin Goose." Technologically ahead of its time, this car was the first to use a self-contained water cooling system to regulate the temperature of the engine. Among its unique features were interchangeable front and rear seats — to reduce wear and tear. Unfortunately, Tucker's company built only 51 cars. Only 48 are still around today.

Tucker's "Tin Goose" really flew! Its top speed was almost 125 miles (200 km) per hour.

This 1944 seaplane prototype was designed to carry 100 passengers and reach speeds of 342 miles (550 km) per hour.

SEAPLANES

Busy planning the new "superliners" of the skies, aircraft designers around the world created planes that would use the sea as a giant runway — but the idea never really took off.

CHOO! CHOO!

Trains were slow to adopt new technologies because the existing machinery was so expensive to replace. Steam engines chugged on into the 1960s in both the United States and Europe. "Big Boy" was the largest, most powerful steam engine ever built. Although only twenty-five were produced (1941–1944), they stayed in service for nearly twenty years before being replaced by the new diesel locomotives.

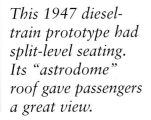

This 1947 diesel-train prototype had split-level seating. Its "astrodome" roof gave passengers a great view.

The Routemaster was more stable than earlier buses. It used less fuel and carried more passengers, too!

SPRUCE GOOSE

On November 2, 1947, the Hughes H-4 Hercules seaplane made its first, and only, flight. This eight-engine machine, nicknamed the *Spruce Goose*, was made of plastic-impregnated wood and was designed to carry 750 passengers. Its designer, Howard Hughes (1905–1976), piloted the plane on a 1-mile (1.6-km) journey in Sacramento, California.

Howard Hughes's Spruce Goose

13

CLASSIC DESIGN

Some vehicle designs took so long to plan that they no longer seemed modern by the time they were finally produced. The famous Routemaster double-decker bus was designed by Douglas Scott (1913–1990) in 1954, but it was not put into service until five years later. By that time, critics complained the bus looked old-fashioned. Even so, buses with this classic design still run on London streets.

THE JET AGE

The modern age of air travel began after World War II. By the end of the 1950s, jet aircraft were the most important means of international travel.

Sir Frank Whittle (right) demonstrates his jet engine to the press in 1948.

FATHER OF THE JET

Englishman Frank Whittle (1907–1996) first thought of the jet engine in 1928, and he built a prototype in 1937. The first jet aircraft to fly, however, was built in Germany by Ernst Heinkel (1888–1958) in 1939. Heinkel learned how to build his jet from Whittle's 1930 patent application. In 1941, a Whittle engine was sent to the United States for use in developing the jet fighter P-80 Shooting Star.

One of the first jet fighters, Gloster Meteor took to the skies in 1944. Hot on its tail was the Messerschmitt Me 262.

14

De Havilland's Comet 4 had round, reinforced windows. The square windows of the Comet 2 were fatally flawed, causing the loss of two planes.

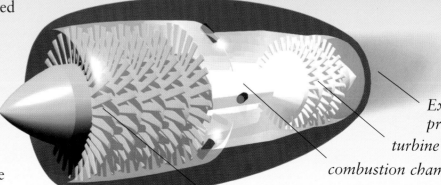

A JET ENGINE

In a jet engine, air is sucked in by a compressor, a series of fan-shaped blades. The compressed air enters a combustion chamber, where it mixes with fuel and ignites, creating an explosion of gases. The gases rush over a turbine, which drives the compressor fans, then jet out the back of the engine with a powerful force that thrusts the plane forward.

Exhaust gases provide thrust.

turbine

combustion chamber

Air is sucked in and compressed.

THE LATEST FLAP

Aircraft designers came up with new ways both to add lift at takeoff and to slow a plane down on landing. Adding adjustable flaps to the wings meant the wings themselves could be smaller. Smaller wings reduced the overall weight of the plane, making flights faster.

MAIDEN VOYAGE

On May 3, 1952, the British Overseas Airways Corporation (BOAC) started the first commercial jet airliner service. The BOAC Comet, designed by the British company de Havilland, flew nearly 6,835 miles (11,000 km), from London to Johannesburg, in less than twenty-four hours, cutting the previous flight time in half.

When the first Boeing 707 rolled off the assembly line in 1957, it was the largest jetliner ever built — more than 98 feet (30 m) long.

CLASSIC PLANE

The first serious competition for the de Havilland Comet was the classic Boeing 707, which took off on December 20, 1957. This plane marked the beginning of the end for great ocean liners, such as the *Queen Mary*. Like the *Queen Mary,* the 707 could carry about 180 passengers across the Atlantic, but the ship cost six times more to build, used ten times more fuel, and was a lot slower.

THE KOREAN WAR

World War II jet fighters came too late to have much impact on that war. The first real jet combat was during the Korean War (1950–1953), with American F-86 Sabres fighting against Soviet MiG-15s. Both had swept-back wings to reduce drag and top speeds of more than 685 miles (1,100 km) an hour.

Although the MiG-15 flew faster, the F-86 was more controllable and proved to be more successful.

LIVING SPACES

During the war, air raids destroyed millions of buildings, and few new ones were being constructed because resources were scarce. When the war ended, however, serious building and rebuilding began.

In 1941, bombs destroyed many terraced homes (right). In 1948, architects took up the challenge to replace them (below).

BRITISH SPIRIT

Architecture seemed to lift people's spirits — more than eight million visited the Royal Festival Hall designed by Leslie Martin (*b*.1908) and Peter Moro (*b*.1911) for the 1951 Festival of Britain. Its classical proportions and the details of its modernist style were inspired by Le Corbusier. Also featured at the festival were the space-age Skylon by Philip Powell (*b*.1921) and Hidalgo Moya (1920–1994) and the Dome of Discovery by Ralph Tubbs (1912–1996).

In 1951, the Dome of Discovery was the largest dome in the world. The latest inventions were on display inside.

HOMES FOR HEROES

Architects also had a more urgent task. Promises of "Homes for Heroes" needed to be met. The solution was applying assembly-line principles to architecture.

PREFAB DESIGN

Le Corbusier (1887–1965) believed in prefabricated, mass-produced, high-rise homes. Inspired by machines, ships, and airplanes, as well as classical architecture, his *Unité d'Habitation* housing, built in Marseilles, France, in 1946–1952, demonstrated his concept of the home as a "machine for living in."

16

BRUTAL BEAUTY

International Style stripped down buildings to their basic elements, usually concrete structures and glass facades. This expressive use of concrete in bold forms was nicknamed "brutalism." By composing buildings with simple units of concrete and glass, architects could use prefabricated materials and build quickly. Richard Neutra (1892–1970) in California and Peter Womersley in Britain placed their buildings carefully in the landscape, then used glass to blur the barriers between interior and exterior space, bringing the outside world inside.

Farnley Hey in Yorkshire, designed by Peter Womersley in 1955, has many large windows to draw the landscape into the living space.

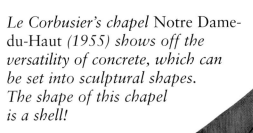

Le Corbusier's chapel Notre Dame-du-Haut (1955) shows off the versatility of concrete, which can be set into sculptural shapes. The shape of this chapel is a shell!

SET IN CONCRETE

Inexpensive concrete was the perfect building material for modernist architects. It could be molded into any shape to create buildings like sculptures. Concrete consists of water, cement, and aggregate (a mixture of sand and gravel). For extra strength, it can be reinforced with steel rods. A technique for reinforcing concrete was developed in France in the 19th century.

17

A network of steel rods is placed in a form, or mold.

Liquid concrete is poured into the mold.

The mold is removed, leaving hardened, reinforced concrete.

Le Corbusier's Unité d'Habitation is the perfect "machine for living in." Raised off the ground on concrete pilotis, it contains more than three hundred fashionable apartments, all with two-story living rooms — plus, shops, a gym, and a rooftop swimming pool!

BUILD IT BIG

International Style became the architectural symbol for the post-war age, especially in the United States. Working with concrete, glass, and steel, architects created organic concrete structures and gleaming glass towers.

The first McDonald's, built in 1955, had instantly recognizable, concrete arches. The company understood the power of a trademark.

NEW YORK GIANT

Soaring skyscrapers were a status symbol. Ludwig Mies van der Rohe (1886–1969) designed the most stunning skyscraper of all, the 38-story Seagram Building (1955–1958). This model of uncompromising beauty is made of glass and bronze-covered steel. Originally, murals of abstract rectangles, by artist Mark Rothko (1903–1970), decorated the inside.

CURVY CONSTRUCT

When designers unveiled a gas station of the future, in 1944, they correctly anticipated the use of prefab concrete in curvy, organic shapes. While stations at the end of the 20th century did have streamlined pumps and, sometimes, restaurants, none had a heliport on the roof!

Futuristic design for a gas station

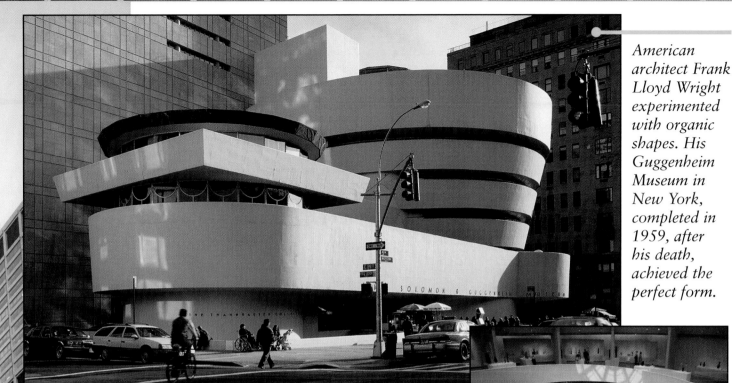

American architect Frank Lloyd Wright experimented with organic shapes. His Guggenheim Museum in New York, completed in 1959, after his death, achieved the perfect form.

Inside the Guggenheim, art hangs along a spiral walkway.

SNAILS AND SAILS

Two of the world's most famous buildings were designed in the 1950s. One is the Guggenheim Museum by Frank Lloyd Wright (1867–1956); the other is the Sydney Opera House by Danish architect Jørn Utzon (b.1918). Both have extraordinary organic shapes. The Guggenheim has a snail-shell facade and spiralling galleries. The harborside Opera House has a roof of billowing, metallic sails.

Although Utzon's plans for the Opera House in Sydney, Australia, were approved in 1956, the project was not completed until 1973.

Depending on the light, the Seagram Building can look like it is made of either black glass or pure bronze.

INTERIORS

During the war, people had more important concerns than decor, so interiors retained the muted greens and browns of the 1930s. After the war, an interest in interiors returned.

INSPIRATION FROM ART

Bold, geometric designs replaced gloomy florals. The artwork of Paul Klee (1879–1940) led to patterns of colored squares on sofas and chairs; the squiggly designs of Joan Miró (1893–1983) were copied on carpets, curtains, and ceramics; and the "drip-and-splash" style of paintings by Jackson Pollock (1912–1956) appeared on wallpapers and textiles.

In an open-plan office (1953), information could be shared freely. Walls were barriers.

20

CONTEMPORARY STYLE

Just as architects wanted to blur the division between inside and outside, interior designers worked to create lighter, airier spaces. By the 1950s, they had abandoned traditional room divisions in homes and offices in favor of open-plan interiors.

FUTURE INTERIOR?

This display from 1956 showed some of the features that might appear in the "living space of the 1980s." At the touch of a button, the dining table rises from the floor, and the chairs fold away when not in use. The designers correctly anticipated remote-control TV, but the hostess cart and the nylon clothes are far more 1950s than 1980s!

A 1950s vision of the interior of the future

The main living area in the California home of designer Charles Eames and his wife, Ray, was an airy, double-story room. The plants and huge windows added to the feeling of space by bringing the outdoors inside.

"Built-ins" replaced freestanding stoves and cabinets in 1950s kitchens.

KNOCKING OUT WALLS

Open-plan interiors were added to existing homes, too. The wall dividing a living room and dining room was often knocked down or replaced with a sliding glass door.

MAKING DO

Do-it-yourself was the solution for those who could not afford to completely transform their homes. Homeowners used a variety of new materials to modernize — especially in kitchens. Formica gave old tabletops a new look; PVC blinds replaced curtains; wipe-clean wallpapers decorated walls; and patterned linoleum covered floors.

In 1958, split-levels defined different living areas.

Open-plan living-dining areas were popular in the 1950s.

FURNITURE

During wartime rationing and even after the war, designers worked to create furniture that was both functional and affordable.

FAIR FURNITURE

In 1941, Britain's Board of Trade started the Utility furniture scheme, which rationed how much furniture was produced and limited the styles available. Only those with a genuine need, such as families whose homes had been bombed, were allowed to buy furniture.

22

MOLDING WOOD

During the war, designers developed new techniques for molding plywood. American Charles Eames (1907–1978) and his wife, Ray (1916–1988), bent and shaped plywood by steaming it against a curved mold. In war years, they made stretchers and leg splints. Later, they used the same molds for fiberglass and plastic.

Movie star Stewart Granger's Hollywood home featured zebra bar stools with tubular-steel legs. The wood veneer TV set was the ultimate luxury.

Fabrics for Utility furniture (1942) came in sensible colors that would hide the dirt. Dining chairs had low backs to save wood.

The prototype of Arne Jacobsen's Ant Chair (1952) was made of molded plywood. Later models were available in bright colors.

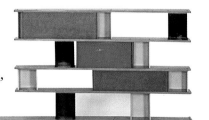

Le Corbusier's influence on French designer Charlotte Perriand can be seen in her colorful "machine for storing books in."

AFFORDABLE FURNITURE

Plywood, fiberglass, and plastic were perfect materials for mass production, which made stylish, well-designed furniture affordable. The first mass-produced plastic chair was Charles Eames's Shell Chair. It was lightweight, durable, and easy to store.

LEGS OF STEEL

Steel rods were a popular choice for chair legs. Danish architect Arne Jacobsen (1902–1971) used them on his famous three-legged Ant Chair. Italian-born sculptor Harry Bertoia (1915–1978) went even further, making his Diamond Chair completely out of steel wire. It was the lightest, airiest chair ever seen!

Although made only of steel wire, Bertoia's Diamond Chair (1952) was expensive because the metal had to be hand-welded.

23

FUNCTION AND FUN

American George Nelson (1908–1986) had a huge influence on furniture design. As head of the Herman Miller furniture company, he created a divider, called the Storage Wall, for open-plan offices. He also designed flexible furniture systems, which were slotted units that fit together for tailor-made storage. Nelson is probably best-remembered, however, for his amazing Marshmallow Sofa. This 3-D sculpture of soft cushions in bright candy colors anticipated the pop art furniture of the next decade.

George Nelson's Marshmallow Sofa (1956) was named for its marshmallow-shaped back and seat cushions. It is one of the first pieces of pop art furniture.

CLASSIC PRODUCTS

The demand for household goods and gadgets and new electrical appliances increased dramatically after the war. With manufacturers using better plastics than ever before, designers created classic products that have barely changed since.

Sold primarily at parties held by home-makers for their friends, Tupperware containers became very popular in the 1950s.

THE TUPPERWARE STORY

In the 1930s, American entrepreneur Earl Tupper invented a flexible, durable, high-quality plastic that, most importantly, was nontoxic and odorless. Tupper used this plastic to make gas masks for the war. After the war, he made food storage containers with a unique, airtight seal that kept food moist in the dry air of the new refrigerators. Tupperware™ was first sold in 1946.

The plastic cases on the new transistor radios came in modern colors, such as pastel pink and lemon yellow.

24

INJECTION MOLDING

screw motor

hopper

plastic pellets

molded plastic

heat

Melted plastic is forced into a cool mold.

Early plastics, such as Bakelite, were thermosetting plastics that could not be reheated and reshaped once they had cooled and set. After the war, a new generation of thermoplastics was developed. Thermoplastics could be reheated and would harden again when cooled. They could also be used in injection molds, which made them well-suited for mass production.

In a screw-injection molding machine, hard pellets of plastic resin flow from a hopper onto a turning screw. Inside the screw, the pellets are heated until they melt. The screw forces the melted plastic into a cool mold, where the plastic quickly hardens. Then the mold springs open, and ejector pins push out the molded plastic.

Parts of a plastic doll are still in this mold. (1951)

ON THE RADIO

Postwar electronic innovations improved portable radios. As transistors and printed circuits replaced vacuum tubes and wires, radios needed less power and could be smaller. Sound quality improved, too, and FM stereo was introduced. International electronics companies, such as Pam and Sony, competed for a share of the U.S. market with "American-style" models in candy-colored, pastel plastics.

CUTTING-EDGE DESIGN

Braun, a German electronics firm, believed that designs should be simple and uncluttered, a style that was known as neofunctionalism. In 1951, the company's best-known designer, Dieter Rams (*b.*1932), created the electric razor, with an oscillating motor in a simple, plastic case.

The Braun electric razor had typical, neofunctional, German styling. This basic design has barely changed.

VACUUM PACT

After World War II, Sixten Sason (1912–1969) designed the perfect modern, streamlined vacuum cleaner for the Electrolux company in Stockholm.

An Electrolux vacuum cleaner (1954) had a flexible hose and attachments that made it more versatile than upright models.

WHAT'S ON TV?

In 1940, there were 10,000 televisions in the United States; by 1958, there were 50 million. Color televisions were first sold at the beginning of the 1950s. By the late 1950s, Sony, a Japanese firm, had already produced a "pocket" model — the TV8-301 transistor television.

A 1954 color television set

HOUSEHOLD DESIGN

Advertising in the 1950s promoted the myth of the perfect housewife-and-hostess, along with the notion that beautifully designed household appliances could make housework a pleasure. According to the ads, using these appliances would give homemakers more leisure time. In reality, housework remained as time-consuming as ever.

TECHNOLOGY AT HOME

Although many homes had electricity installed during the 1930s, electrical appliances did not become common until after the war. Then, homemakers could have electric washing machines, vacuum cleaners, space heaters, kettles, stoves, and refrigerators. The electric home was fast becoming a reality. During the 1950s, many families also had their first telephones installed.

CLASSIC KETTLE

In 1959, as plug-in electric kettles were replacing the stove-top kind, William Russell designed the K2 kettle for Russell Hobbs. The K2 was part of Hobbs's "Forgettable" line of products with automatic shut-off switches. This feature was a huge improvement over earlier electric kettles that just kept boiling until they burned out.

The K2 could boil water in seconds, and it featured a cool-touch handle and lid knob. Most importantly, it turned itself off when the water boiled.

THE FIRST MICROWAVE

Radar, developed during World War II, used invisible energy waves to detect enemy planes, but scientist Percy Spencer discovered that radar microwaves also melted the chocolate bar in his pocket. Raytheon's radar range was the first oven to use these microwaves. When it came on the market in 1947, the radar range caused a sensation — it cooked a hamburger in 35 seconds — but with a price tag of $3,000, it cost more than a family house!

CLEAN LINES

Designers in the United States led the way in styling new household appliances. Industrial designers, such as Raymond Loewy, applied the same streamlined look to refrigerators as they did to automobiles, producing a modern, curvy style. The latest designs all shared one common feature — they were sleek. Keeping homes clean became easier as homeowners purchased built-in kitchen fixtures and installed wall-to-wall carpets.

In the 1950s, kitchens became sleeker, and built-in fixtures made them easier to keep clean.

The Kenwood food mixer, designed by Kenneth Grange in the 1940s, featured attachments still used today. Early models even had a buffer for polishing silverware!

PAYING THE PRICE

Household products were popular purchases, and people bought even more of them after the introduction of installment buying. Instead of paying for products right away, buyers could take them home and pay a little each week.

This clever chilled-water dispenser first appeared on refrigerator doors in the 1950s. It would become stylish again near the end of the century.

FASHION

Clothing designs, especially in women's wear, changed significantly during the 1940s and 1950s.

WARTIME AUSTERITY

In the United States, L85 laws controlled the use of wool and silk during the war. In Britain, the government asked top designers to produce a basic "Utility" wardrobe, using as little fabric as possible. Manufacturers had to be specially licensed to mass-produce this clothing, which quickly became known for its high quality.

Britain's Utility wardrobe was unveiled in 1942. Utility clothes were sensible and durable.

In the United States, oversized zoot suits scornfully disregarded wartime laws.

28

A NEW LOOK

Femininity returned in 1947, when French designer Christian Dior (1905–1957) unveiled his New Look. Sloping shoulders, a pinched waist, and a full skirt produced a curvy, hourglass silhouette. Some women loved the elegance of the look; others refused to get back into their corsets to wear it! Critics complained that, with raw materials still in short supply, the style wasted too much fabric.

Designer Claire McCardell pioneered mass production as a way of creating comfortable, affordable clothing.

This 1947 Dior design has an hourglass silhouette. The wool coat opens to reveal a pleated taffeta skirt.

DRESSING FOR COMFORT

Women seeking a more relaxed look wore clothes by American designers. Clothes by Claire McCardell (1905–1958) were sporty, comfortable, and functional.

McCardell used ordinary fabrics, such as cotton, jersey, and denim. Most of her clothes, including her wraparound skirt, were separates designed to be mixed and matched.

The twinset — a knit top with a matching cardigan — and the wraparound skirt were popular styles in the 1950s.

THE RISE OF YOUTH COUTURE

By the late 1950s, baby boomers (babies born just after the war) had grown into teenagers. Inspired by novels and movies to develop their own styles, teenage rebels wore jeans, T-shirts, and leather jackets, while moody beatniks blurred the lines between male and female styles. By the 1960s, however, these "anti-fashions" were high fashion. Youth styles dominated couture.

THE NYLON REVOLUTION

Nylon, the first synthetic fabric, was patented by DuPont in 1937. It was easy to dye, and the color did not fade. It had a silky feel but did not wrinkle or attract moths. Nylon transformed the textile industry and was soon being mixed with natural fibers to make dresses, suits, ties, and undergarments, especially nylon stockings. Nylon stockings first went on sale in the United States in May 1940. They sold out in four days!

nylon chips

hopper

Nylon chips are heated to make a viscous fluid.

Cold air hardens the nylon thread.

Hot steam sets, or fixes, the thread.

Nylon is forced through a spinneret.

Nylon filaments are twisted into yarn and wound onto a bobbin.

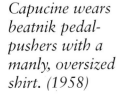

French model Capucine wears beatnik pedal-pushers with a manly, oversized shirt. (1958)

Nylon stockings are shaped on metal frames.

· TIME LINE ·

	DESIGN	WORLD EVENTS	TECHNOLOGY	FAMOUS PEOPLE	ART & MEDIA
1940		•World War II continues (1939–1945)	•U.S.: first nylon stockings on sale	•Paul Klee dies	•Stravinsky: Symphony in C major
1941	•Utility scheme furniture	•Japanese attack Pearl Harbor; U.S. enters war	•Big Boy locomotive built •Terylene thread invented	•Marriage of Charles and Ray Eames	•Brecht: Mother Courage •Coward: Blithe Spirit
1942	•Curtiss Kittyhawk	•Oxfam founded	•Soft toilet paper introduced in Britain	•Gandhi imprisoned by British in India	•Bergman and Bogart star in Casablanca
1943		•Mussolini arrested •Zoot suit riots in U.S.	•Britain: Colossus computer		•Sartre: Being and Nothingness
1944		•Allies land in France and drive back Germans		•Glenn Miller dies in plane crash	•Henry Moore: Mother and Child
1945		•Germany and Japan surrender; war ends	•First atomic bombs •Microwave oven patented	•U.S.: Truman elected President •Suicide of Hitler	•Britten: Peter Grimes •Steinbeck: Cannery Row
1946	•Vespa motor scooter	•UN General Assembly holds first meetings	•ENIAC computer built •Tupperware launched		•Picasso: Reclining Nude •O'Neill: The Iceman Cometh
1947	•LEGOs go on sale •Dior: New Look	•India and Pakistan gain independence	•Yeager breaks sound barrier in U.S. Bell X-1	•Howard Hughes pilots Spruce Goose	•Cannes Film Festival opens •Camus: The Plague
1948	•Citroën 2CV •Tucker:"Tin Goose"	•S. Africa: apartheid begins •Israel proclaimed	•Michelin: radial tire •Transistor invented	•Gandhi assassinated	•Huston: Key Largo •John Wayne in Red River
1949	•De Havilland: Comet •Loewy on cover of Time	•NATO formed •East and West Germany formed		•Mao proclaims Chinese People's Republic	•Orwell: 1984
1950	•Loewy: Studebaker	•Korean War begins •China invades Tibet	•Gas turbine car (Rover)	•U.S.: McCarthyism begins	•Miró: mural for Harvard •Pollock: Autumn Rhythm
1951	•Festival of Britain		•First video recording •Braun electric razor		•The African Queen
1952	•Unité d'Habitation •Jacobsen: Ant Chair	•Kenya: Mau Mau revolt begins		•Elizabeth II proclaimed Queen of Britain	
1953	•Chevrolet uses fiberglass reinforcement	•Korean War ends •Egypt: Nasser in power	•Crick and Watson describe DNA structure	•Hillary and Norgay climb Mt. Everest	•Osborne: Look Back in Anger •Miller: The Crucible
1954	•Boeing 707 •Univers typeface	•SEATO formed	•Atomic tests at Bikini Atoll	•Roger Bannister runs four-minute mile	•Kingsley Amis: Lucky Jim •Brando in The Wild One
1955	•Citroën DS •Le Corbusier: Notre Dame-du-Haut	•Warsaw Pact •South Africa leaves UN	•Hovercraft patented •Optical fibers patented	•Einstein dies •Jackson Pollock dies	•Patrick White: Tree of Man •Hitchcock: Rear Window
1956	•IBM logo •Sydney Opera House designed	•Suez Crisis in Middle East	•Britain: first commercial nuclear power station	•Elvis Presley's Heartbreak Hotel tops U.S. record chart	•Allen Ginsberg: Howl •Beckett: Waiting for Godot
1957		•EEC (Common Market) founded	•USSR launches first satellite, Sputnik 1	•Macmillan succeeds Eden as British prime minister	•Kerouac: On the Road •Chagall: The Circus Rider
1958	•Seagram Building •Holtom: CND logo	•CND starts anti-bomb protests	•Heart pacemaker invented	•De Gaulle elected president of France	•Chevalier and Caron star in Gigi
1959	•Austin Mini •Guggenheim completed	•Cuba: Castro in power •U.S. troops sent to Laos	•Silicon chips •DuPont: Lycra	•Buddy Holly dies in plane crash	

GLOSSARY

bubble car: a class of economical, fuel-efficient microcars that, with only three wheels, were a kind of cross between a car and a motor scooter.

flap: a movable metal slat, or airfoil, along the back edge of an airplane's wing, used to increase lift or drag; agitated excitement.

logo: a symbol designed to represent the name of a product or a company in an easy-to-recognize, graphic way.

New Look: the name given to Christian Dior's 1947 collection, which offered a change from practical wartime clothing to more feminine fashions characterized by an hourglass silhouette. Later, the term also referred to modern furniture and ceramics.

organic: resembling a living thing from nature; often used to describe designs with curvy shapes.

oscillating: swinging; moving back and forth.

pilotis: strong, supporting pillars or columns that raise a building above the ground to a second-story level.

propaganda: ideas spread purposely to gain support for a cause or to damage or defeat an opposing cause.

prototype: an original model of a product, which is subsequently copied to mass-produce the product.

PVC: the abbreviation for "polyvinyl chloride," which is a synthetic plastic material.

rationed: distributed as an allowance or a share of the total supply available.

synthetic: artificially produced, often by using chemicals, especially to imitate something that occurs naturally.

typographer: a designer who creates or selects typefaces for printing.

viscous: semi-fluid, thick, or sticky; resistant to flow.

MORE BOOKS TO READ

The 40s & 50s: Utility to New Look. 20th Century Fashion (series). Helen Reynolds (Gareth Stevens)

The 1950s. Cultural History of the United States Through the Decades (series). Stuart A. Kallen, editor (Lucent Books)

America's Favorite Architects. Discover (series). Patricia Brown Glenn (John Wiley & Sons)

Automobiles. History (series). David Corbett (Barrons Juveniles)

A Golden Age: The Golden Age of Radio. Martha Wickham (Soundprints Corporation)

Hiroshima and Nagasaki. New Perspectives (series). R.G. Grant (Raintree/Steck-Vaughn)

Mid-Century Modern: Furniture of the 1950s. Cara Greenberg (Harmony Books)

Nuclear Power. 20th Century Inventions (series). Nina Morgan (Raintree/Steck-Vaughn)

Television. Inventors & Inventions (series). Janet Riehecky (Benchmark Books)

Tupperware: The Promise of Plastic in 1950s America. Alison J. Clarke (Smithsonian Institution Press)

WEB SITES

Eames Office: Eames Design FAQ&A. *www.eamesoffice.com*

HK-1 History: "Spruce Goose" history page. *sprucegoose.org/sprucegoose/history/history1.htm*

The Midtown Book: The Seagram Building. *www.thecityreview.com/park375.html*

The Tucker Automobile Pages. *www.tuckerclub.org*

Due to the dynamic nature of the Internet, some web sites stay current longer than others. To find additional web sites, use a reliable search engine with one or more of the following keywords: *aircraft, architecture, Citroën, Dior, Electrolux, Le Corbusier, locomotives, Raymond Loewy, nylon, television, transistor radio, Tupperware, Utility scheme,* and *Vespa.*

INDEX